JAMES STEVENSON

I Meant to Tell You

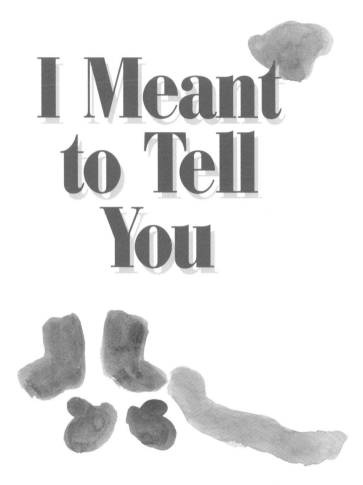

GREENWILLOW BOOKS, NEW YORK

To Suçie, Jane,
Wina, and Emma,
with love

Printed in Hong Kong by South China Printing Company (1988) Ltd.
First Edition   10 9 8 7 6 5 4 3 2 1

Library of Congress Cataloging-in-Publication Data

Stevenson, James, (date)
I meant to tell you / by James Stevenson.
      p.   cm.
Summary: The author remembers special times that
he and his daughter shared as she was growing up.
ISBN 0-688-14177-3 (trade).   ISBN 0-688-14178-1 (lib. bdg.)
1. Stevenson, James (date)—Family—Juvenile literature.
2. Authors, American—20th century—Biography—Juvenile literature.
3. Illustrators—United States—Biography—Juvenile literature.
4. Fathers and daughters—United States—Juvenile literature.
[1. Stevenson, James (date).   2. Authors, American.
3. Illustrators.   4. Fathers and daughters.]   I. Title.
PS3569.T4557Z4767   1996
813'.54—dc20   [B]   95-5463   CIP   AC

I meant to tell you, before I forget:
I remember when you were small.

I remember walking down the sidewalk with you,
holding your hand.

I remember some nights,
when you were small,
you never went to sleep.

I remember how you laughed
when I threw flapjacks in the air.

I remember leaving you at nursery school
and having to drive away.

I loved the pictures
you brought home.

You went to dance class after school.
(I thought you were the best.)

I remember we brought
Sarah home in a shoebox.

When Sarah got big,
you used her as a pillow.

We went to the beach when the waves were big
and the rain was warm.

You collected lots of things.

ROCKS

SEA GLASS

SHELLS

LEAVES

FEATHERS

We made castles in the sand and tunnels
that let in the sea.

You said Sarah was the princess in the castle.

You didn't mind when the wave came
and washed it all away.

You rode a camel at the zoo

and watched big sharks go by at the aquarium.

One day we drove two hours
through the rain to see a rodeo.

They roped a calf.
You burst into tears.

We drove back home again.

When I was working,
you would ask me what I was doing.

I gave you paper and crayons.
You worked, too.

Sometimes we found a strip of birch bark in the woods.
We pretended it was a letter from the Indians.

"How are you?" it said.
"We hope you are fine.
   Your friends, the Indians."

You made houses out of cardboard boxes.

TRY AND
FIND ME

We picked tomatoes from the garden.

You learned not to be afraid
to jump off the dock.

You knew that I'd catch you.

The first time you rode your bike alone,

you went faster and faster and couldn't stop.

You went down a hill and into a hedge.

You were scared when you came out of the hedge,
but not for long.

You kept on going. I was very proud.

One day in the park when I was sad,
you put your arm around me.

You said you wanted to show me
how fast you could run.

You raced by,
your head turned toward me,
watching to see if I was watching.

We got a pumpkin every Halloween.
It took a long time to find the right one.

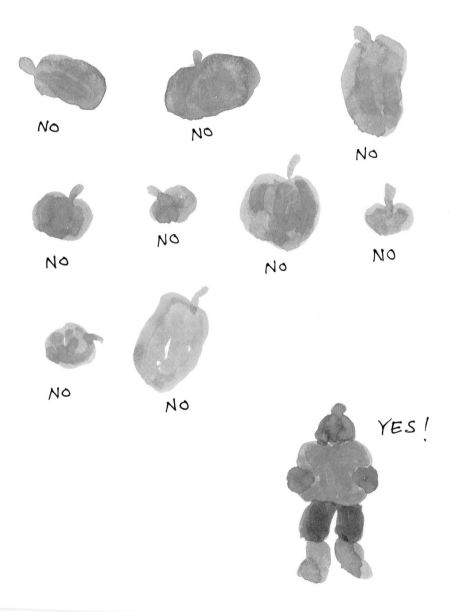

When it snowed, we played board games
and listened to music.

It was a while ago. . . .

But I remember you when you were small
and all the things we did together.
I meant to tell you that.